Chimenti: Michelangelo showing
a project to Leo X.
Florence: Casa Buonarroti

tebuoni: The meeting between Julius II
 Michelangelo in Bologna.
ence: Casa Buonarroti

Boschi: Michelangelo presenting
a model to Julius II.
Florence: Casa Buonarroti

General Editor
DR ENZO ORLANDI

Text by
MARIA LUISA RIZZATTI

Translator
C.J. RICHARDS

Copyright © MCMLXVI
by Arnoldo Mondadori Editore
Library of Congress
Catalog Card Number: 75 - 528
All rights reserved.
This edition is published
by Crescent Books,
a division of Crown Publishers, Inc.
by arrangement with
Arnoldo Mondadori Editore

ISBN: 0-517-163047

Printed in Italy by
Arnoldo Mondadori Editore - Verona

THE LIFE, TIMES AND ART OF

MICHELANGELO

CRESCENT BOOKS - NEW YORK

A WILD AND SOLITARY YOUTH

The two predominant traits in Michelangelo's character, solitariness and wildness, were symbolically present at his birth. The village where he was born, Caprese in Valtiberina, was solitary and wild, on the steep slope of a hill amid oaks, chestnut trees and fields. The house still stands, perched above the village, a rustic mansion, decorated with coats of arms, where the mayors of Florence lived for the six months of their tenure. This office had fallen to the lot of Lodovico Buonarroti during the first half of 1475 and there, on March 6, was born a male child whom he named Michelangelo. Very little is known about the mother. Her name was Francesca di Miniato del Sera. She was 18 or 20 years old when she gave birth to her second son and died in 1481 shortly after the birth of her fifth one, leaving Lodovico available for a new matrimonial venture into which he soon plunged. The Buonarroti were a family of solid burgher and artisan stock whose ancestry could be traced back two centuries. In later years a genealogy for the Buonarroti was conjured up which claimed among its forebears the Counts of Canossa and, through them, the imperial house of Canossa; but this was an unsubstantiated connection which came to light only after Michelangelo had become a famous artist. A certain Count Alexander of Canossa suddenly discovered he was related to him and invited him to become acquainted with "your relations and your house." The strangest aspect of this story is that Michelangelo took it seriously. Genius sometimes has these foibles: Even Dante confessed to caring about his aristocratic origins, but those, at least, were authentic. However, Michelangelo remembered with an equal pride his wet nurse in Settignano, wife of a stone cutter, and declared that with her milk he had also "received the knack of handling chisel and hammer." There was no affection between himself and his father, who lived to a very advanced age. At first Lodovico disapproved of his son's vocation in the arts, because he looked upon it as a mechanical activity, a form of manual labor. To become a merchant seemed to him to be a much more distinguished occupation. It was only when he discovered that the paint brush and the chisel could be lucrative that the one-time mayor forgave his son for having disqualified himself socially. He was a querulous, unsociable, stingy man. Yet Michelangelo must have felt some sentiment for him, because in a letter he wrote to him in 1516, he said, "All the troubles I have borne, I have borne out of affection for you."

Opposite page: This well known portrait of Michelangelo, ascribed by some to Jacopino del Conto, and thought by others to be a self-portrait, was painted around 1540 when Michelangelo was 65. It shows clearly his deformed nose, broken in his adolescence by a jealous fellow student, Pietro Torrigiani. But even more apparent is his sadness and weariness. Left: The Nicodemus of the Pietà (Deposition from the Cross) in Santa Maria del Fiore, the Cathedral of Florence. This is probably a self-portrait of the sculptor. Below: Another portrait of Michelangelo by a Florentine disciple of his who worked with him when he was painting the frescoes on the ceiling of the Sistine Chapel. In this portrait Michelangelo is still relatively serene and young.

THE FLORENCE OF THE MEDICI

Michelangelo's happiest years had as a background the Florence of Lorenzo the Magnificent, a city refined, devout, intellectual and dedicated to the enjoyment of life. Political power was firmly in the hands of the Medici, those 15th-century merchant princes who had become the masters of Florence by a progressive and astute manipulation of public affairs. There had been no plutocrats in the Middle Ages: The coming to power of the Medici was a sign of new times. Henceforth it would be money that waged war and peace; it would be the determining factor in many other fields as well. In Lorenzo de' Medici, who came to power at a very early age, were revived the genius and open-mindedness of his grandfather Cosimo who had founded the political fortunes of the family. Cosimo had not changed any part of the republic's structure. On the contrary, he had become its jealous guardian; but key positions, although elective, somehow always found their way into the hands of his supporters. The great families of Florence had tried in vain to eliminate him, first putting him into prison, and then banishing him from the city. But financiers have a way of getting out of tight spots.

The seemingly easy-going lordship of the Medicis, attended as it was by their liberality, was popular with the majority of Florentines in whom the memory of the disorders of the Commune (a species of self-government prevalent in many Italian cities during the Middle Ages and the early Renaissance) was still fresh. They provided countless feasts, pageants, carnivals for the populace, munificently rewarding participants in all kinds of contests of poetry, painting, sculpture, architecture, and music. They encouraged art, supported the Church, at least by adding to its buildings and their decoration, and lavishly entertained a steady stream of distinguished visitors in the palace on the via Larga. Lorenzo, who had been left in sole power after the assassination of his brother Giuliano on the tragic Easter of 1478 (a last outburst of opposition engineered by the great families: the Pazzi, the Pitti and the Salviati), made of his patronage of the arts a weapon of government. As a poet, he proffered in charming verse an invitation to practical paganism: "Who would be happy, let him be; of tomorrow who can say?"—a piece of advice that was echoed and re-echoed a century later by French and English poets: "Gather ye rosebuds while ye may . . ." Even this warning of Lorenzo's to enjoy the fleeing hour shows political acumen; revelers are never dangerous adversaries. It is not surprising that opposition, when it took hold, came in the form of a Dominican monk whose face was ravaged by fasts and wrinkled by long hours of vigil—Girolamo Savonarola. But the hour of revolt had not yet rung: Lorenzo was to die in bed in 1492, the year America was discovered. According to a popular account, Savonarola, summoned to his death bed, refused to grant him absolution.

Opposite: Benozzo Gozzoli's "Journey of the Magi." The artist painted the background and procession to Bethlehem with a wealth of color. He took his inspiration from the pageants which were held in Florence to celebrate Twelfth Night, casting the Medici in the roles of the Wise Men. It is thought that the handsome youth on the white charger is Lorenzo; Cosimo, soberly dressed in blue, follows on a mule. Other members of the Medici court are also portrayed.

Above: The Medici Palace as it appeared in the 16th century. It was begun by Michelozzo in 1444 for Cosimo the Elder.

The two preceding pages show an idealized picture of the Medici and the members of their court. Here they are shown as they probably looked in every-day life. These portraits were painted by Michelangelo's first teacher, Domenico Ghirlandaio, who was essentially a fresco painter and who contributed immeasurably to the development of that art. From left to right: The three boys are Giovanni, Piero and Giuliano de' Medici. In the middle: The poet Agnolo Poliziano. Then the humanists: Marsilio Ficino, Cristoforo Landino, Poliziano again, and Gentile de' Becchi, Lorenzo the Magnificent's teacher. The three Vespucci: Amerigo the Elder, Amerigo the Younger, Simonetta, beloved of Giuliano de' Medici. Giovanni Argiropulo, a Greek scholar famous in his day. Below, from left to right: A group of nobles of the Tornabuoni, Populeschi and Giachinotti families; three ladies of the court, the eldest being Lorenzo's mother. Three more ladies of the Albizzi and Soderini families. Then, between Antonio Pucci and Francesco Sassetti, Lorenzo the Magnificent. The last four are members of the Ghirlandaio family.

A GARDEN OF STONE

It was in a garden that Michelangelo first found the world in which he wanted to live, a garden of stones filled with broken pillars and truncated columns and inhabited by statues with large, vacant eyes. This was the garden of San Marco, a kind of open-air art academy where Cosimo the Elder and later Piero and then Lorenzo de' Medici collected ancient and modern sculpture. Here, a few young men practiced art under the guidance of a pupil of Donatello's, master Bertoldo. Michelangelo's precocious skill in the modeling of a pleasingly realistic faun's head aroused the interest of Lorenzo the Magnificent, always on the lookout for young talent. From then on the shy young man, who had been considered by his family as something of a black sheep, was treated like a son by the lord of Florence. He was then 15. During the two remaining years of Lorenzo's life the boy lived in the palace on the via Larga where he was assigned a room, suitable clothes, a monthly allowance of five florins, and a place at the table next to Lorenzo's sons. It was an unforgettable experience not because of the reflected glory—Michelangelo was always to remain indifferent to this sort of distinction—but because of the new world that was revealed to him by the group of brilliant intellectuals whom Lorenzo had gathered about him: Poliziano, Sandro Botticelli, Marsilio Ficino, Pico della Mirandola. These men, with their eagerness for research, their passionate cult of beauty, now became Michelangelo's teachers. Ghirlandaio, in whose shop he had briefly served as an apprentice, was already part of his past. Michelangelo now turned to vigorous, dramatic old masters, Giotto and Masaccio, in whose frescoes he sought the secret of plasticity in figures. From then on he judged the quality of a painting by the relief given the figures. And it was in the Masaccio chapel in the church of the Carmine in Florence, where he had gone to study the frescoes, that he got into a fight with Pietro Torrigiani, who

marked him for life with a blow on the nose. Michelangelo was not handsome, and this accident filled him with bitterness. Torrigiani later boasted of it: "I felt that bone and cartilage smash under my fist as though they had been wafers."

Another of his inspirations was the powerful painting of Luca Signorelli. His frescoes in the Cathedral of Orvieto which illustrate the final destiny of man—death, judgment, heaven and hell—remained in his mind like a vision full of vigor which was to be reechoed later in his grandiose conception of the "Last Judgment." The plasticity of Luca's painting—with its dynamic twistings of the damned, of devils, of the elect—also fascinated Michelangelo. Slowly he became convinced that painting and sculpture are fundamentally the same thing.

The death of Lorenzo the Magnificent when he was only 44 years old brought about a complete reversal in Michelangelo's circumstances. Condivi, one of his contemporary biographers, wrote that "for many days he was unable to do anything."

Like a wounded animal returning to his lair, Michelangelo left a court submerged in mourning and returned to his father's house in the via Bentaccordi. Never again would there be the affection and understanding between him and the Medici that had existed in the days of the Magnificent. Piero, the new lord of Florence, did not think to summon Michelangelo to the palace on the via Larga for six months. On a winter's day he remembered about him and asked him to make a giant snowman in the courtyard. The snow giant melted but had appealed so much to Lorenzo's son that Michelangelo all at once came back into favor and became, in the eyes of Piero, one of the outstanding personages in Florence. Michelangelo, proud and touchy as he was, never forgave earlier slights. His dislike of the Medici continued unabated to his death.

Far left: Detail of a fresco by Giotto in the Peruzzi Chapel in Santa Croce in Florence (Episodes in the life of St. John the Baptist). This cycle belongs to the later works of the master and differs from the Assisi and Padua works in its greater stylistic incisiveness. Left: A copy by Michelangelo of the same detail. Giotto also painted a "Last Judgment" in Padua.

Left: Detail in Masaccio's fresco in the Brancacci Chapel in the Church of the Carmine in Florence, depicting "The Tribute Money," which is part of the life of Saint Peter. The artist worked at it from 1427 to the beginning of 1428.
Below left: A drawing by Michelangelo which copies

Masaccio's painting of Saint Peter handing the coin to the sailor. Below right: This painting, by Luca Signorelli, clearly inspired, with its sculptural overtones the figure of the judging Christ (left) which Michelangelo painted in the center of the altar wall of the Sistine Chapel in his fresco of the "Last Judgment."

CLASSICAL INFLUENCES

The ancient statues in the Medici garden of San Marco had exerted a deep, long-lasting influence on Michelangelo's spirit. Sculpture was to remain his primary interest even though it became increasingly evident to him that there is often no clear line of demarcation between sculpture and painting. Although times and circumstances forced him to become architect, engineer and painter as well, he was always to consider these activities as secondary. While he was painting the frescoes on the vaulted ceiling of the Sistine Chapel, he continued to refer to himself, perversely, as "Michelangelo, sculptor in Rome." He sought the mystery of classical perfection in the statues of antiquity. Influenced by memories of conversations he had heard at the court of Lorenzo the Magnificent, between the philosopher Marsilio Ficino and his followers, he began to look upon the human body as the highest creation of God, a proof of His perfection. This was in sharp contrast to the medieval concept of the human body as a repository of evil and sin, whose flesh was to be scorned and mortified. He began in earnest to study the nude, not only in ancient statues but in fresh corpses. The prior of Santo Spirito had given him a den in an Augustinian hospital for the poor where Michelangelo spent long hours dissecting cadavers. It was in this crude anatomy laboratory that he spent nauseous, haunting nights, discovering the network of muscles and tendons which were later to play such an important part in his masterpieces. But this ghoulish course of study cast a pall over his spirit and affected his digestion.

THE CHOICE BETWEEN GOOD AND EVIL

Michelangelo's first contact with the work of Jacopo della Quercia, the finest sculptor of the first half of the 15th century, took place in Bologna where the youthful artist had fled. This was the first of many such flights in the course of his life. In 1494 the army of Charles VIII of France arrived at the very gates of Florentine territory after Gerolamo Savonarola from his pulpit in the cathedral had announced the coming of divine punishment. The voice of the monk blew on Michelangelo like a fiery wind. Savonarola thundered against the Medici, the tyrants of Florence, with their empty splendor and their reign of worldly vanities. In his old age Michelangelo was to say that he could still hear the terrifying voice of the preacher. At the announcement of impending doom, the youthful Buonarroti took flight: from Florence to Venice and thence to Bologna. In this latter city, in the bas-reliefs of the doors of San Petronio, the strong personality of Jacopo della Quercia was revealed to him. Here, with a fresh spirit, in revolt against medieval tradition, are depicted the great Biblical subjects which Michelangelo was to make his own in the decoration of the Sistine Chapel: the creation of Adam, the expulsion from the Garden of Eden, the Prophets. The young Florentine fugitive meditated for a long time on the lessons learned from Jacopo, placing him, in his mind, side by side with his favorite painter, Masaccio. Their interpretations of the casting out of Adam and Eve from the Garden of Eden express the same tragic quality inherent in a subject with which Michelangelo was also obsessed. The man of the Renaissance becomes aware of his own freedom in the choice between Good and Evil. And it is the consciousness of having chosen Evil which makes Eve, in Masaccio's painting (left), open her dark mouth in a howl of anguish, and makes Adam twist his limbs as he is prodded by the Angel in Jacopo's bas-relief (see upper right). These images left an indelible imprint on Michelangelo's mind, preoccupied as he was with eternal problems. It is apparent even in the works of his early youth that Christian inspiration was present within him side by side with the pagan. From the classics he learned the rules of external perfection; but the spiritual content of his works—the sublimation of grief, faith in justice, the glorification of liberty—sprang from the highest values of Christianity.

On this page and the next one are three interpretations of the same subject:
The expulsion of Adam and Eve from the Garden of Eden.
Left: Masaccio's dramatic fresco in the Brancacci Chapel in the Church of the Carmine in Florence.
Above: Jacopo della Quercia's bas-relief on the door of the Church of San Petronio in Bologna.

Right: Michelangelo's interpretation in a fresco on the ceiling of the Sistine Chapel.
In Bologna, where he first came into contact with the work of Jacopo della Quercia, Michelangelo executed a candelabrum held up by an angel and two statues of lesser dimensions: Saint Petronius and Saint Proculus. He was barely 20 when he was in Bologna.
When he returned to Florence in 1495 (Piero de' Medici had fled ingloriously before the invading troops of Charles VIII of France), Michelangelo found the city had once more become a republic.

WAS THIS THE FACE
OF HIS MOTHER?

The urge to glorify man, so marked among the princes of the Renaissance, found its highest expression in the building of magnificent tombs. Christians in name only, they all aspired to make of their final place of rest a monument to last for all eternity—one which would remind posterity of their glory. This attitude of Michelangelo's patrons toward death explains why he drew up so many grandiose plans for sepulchral monuments. These were to absorb him all his life. His youthful "Pietà" in St. Peter's was intended to adorn a tomb. It was commissioned by the French Cardinal, Jean Bilhères de Lagraulas, who had come to Italy in the retinue of Charles VIII and who had then stayed on at the papal court. Like all his compatriots, the cardinal was obsessed with "grandeur." After he had left the world of the living, his monument was to serve as a reminder of his own and his nation's glory. In the autumn of 1497 a Roman patron of the arts, Jacopo Galli, presented the 22-year-old Michelangelo to the prelate, assuring him that he would fashion "the most beautiful work in marble in Rome." However, the Frenchman never had the satisfaction of seeing it completed. He died on August 6, 1499. Perhaps the terrible recollection of the torture of Savonarola, burned at the stake in Florence by his political enemies in 1498, hovered over Michelangelo as he sculptured this "Pietà." Some saw in the face of Mary, "so young, so Florentine, so sad," a reflection of the features of Francesca Buonarroti, the mother whom he had lost so soon and hardly known.

Above: The "Pietà" in St. Peter's in Rome. This was the first treatment of a subject which Michelangelo was to take up at various times right up to his death. Right: Detail of the ribbon, which runs from the Virgin's left shoulder to her right hip across her breast, on which is carved the sculptor's name. He added it at night, after the statue was unveiled, because he had heard some Lombard pilgrims say that it was the work of Cristoforo Solari. Opposite: The back of the "Pietà."

*Above: The "Holy Family," also known as the "Doni Madonna," at the Uffizi Gallery in Florence. It was painted probably in 1503 for the wedding of Agnolo Doni and Maddalena Strozzi. Doni, who had made his fortune in woolen textiles, wanted a portrait by Raphael (who also did one of his wife) and a sacred picture by Michelangelo, to whom he agreed to pay 70 ducats. But when the painting was delivered, he tried to settle for only 40. The artist, infuriated, sent him word that he would take back the painting unless Doni, in compensation, paid him twice the sum originally agreed on.
The merchant had to comply.
Right: Plaster cast of the original "Taddei Madonna" which is at the Royal Academy, London.
Opposite page: The "Pitti Madonna" which is in the Bargello, Florence. These names come from the original owners. In both of these bas-reliefs, especially in the "Pitti Madonna," the figure of Mary is reminiscent of ancient sculptures of the Sybils, while the Child has the same vivacity as certain putti (cupidlike infants) on classical funerary monuments.*

MICHELANGIOLO BUONARROTI
1475 - 1564
LA VERGINE COL FIGLIO E S. GIOVANNI

A FRIENDSHIP
OF TITANS

In 1505, after a four years' stay, Michelangelo left Tuscany (where he had carved the powerful "David" and a few severe madonnas) and returned to Rome. The recently elected pontiff, Julius II, wanted him to build his tomb. Julius II was the perfect example of a Renaissance prince: He was a great lord, a brave warrior, a patron of the arts. His tomb was to be a mausoleum befitting a Pope who had wanted to surround himself with the finest talent his century had to offer. The greatest architect, Bramante, was to rebuild St. Peter's for him; the most delicate painter, Raphael, was to decorate his palace; and now the ablest sculptor, Michelangelo, was to fashion his tomb. The two, Pope and sculptor, understood each other. They had the same passionate and fiery temperament. They knew nothing of simple things, they thought only in gigantic terms. And their friendship, through all its vicissitudes, was indeed a friendship of Titans.

Below: Details from two of the nine central panels of the ceiling of the Sistine Chapel. Michelangelo bestows on even the lowliest mortals performing the humblest of tasks a grandiose solemnity.
Left: Fugitives from the "Deluge" bearing their goods and chattels.
Right: Firewood carried to the furnace for "The Sacrifice of Noah."
Opposite page: The same muscular treatment is given the figures in "The Fall of Man." The contract for the painting of the frescoes on the ceiling of the Sistine Chapel was signed in May, 1508. Under its terms, Michelangelo was to cover the ceiling, which had originally been tinted a light blue dotted with yellow stars, with giant figures of the 12 Apostles. However, as soon as the artist had seen the

Chapel, the 12 Apostles were forgotten, and he conceived a magnificent design. In his mind's eye he saw the Chapel expanded into a universe in which noble figures were composed in a fantastic harmony. Down the center of the vault there were to be nine panels representing the Creation and the Fall of Man from Grace. In the triangular spaces below, Prophets and Sybils were to be shown. The remainder of the spaces were crowded with colossal figures within a complex frame of simulated architecture. Ironically, despite both his reluctance to undertake the work and his resistance to painting as a medium, the decoration of the Sistine Chapel was the only work in all his life which he was able to complete as he had planned it.

COLOSSUS BETWEEN MOUNTAINS AND SKY

The "tragedy of the tomb" (the Pope's) was destined to drag on for 40 years. There were misunderstandings, quarrels, flights, changes in the design, grudges and outbursts of temper first with Julius II, then with his successors and his heirs. And yet Michelangelo owed to the uncompleted tomb some of the greatest moments of his creative activity. For it he returned to the wild solitude of the Apuan Alps, which he had already visited at the time of the "Pietà" to excavate blocks of marble. Again his imagination was captured by the mystery of the forms imprisoned in those dazzling blocks. The Apuan Alps were a fitting background for him, an immense stage setting: he dreamed of carving here between mountains and sky a colossus so tall that sailors in their ships, far from the shores, would be able to see it. This statue was never made. He was requested, instead, to make a different type of colossus. This was the penance imposed upon him by Julius II

after a quarrel and the sculptor's subsequent flight, which kept him from the Papal court for seven months. During that period he had even thought of getting himself invited by the Sultan Bajezid and emigrating to Turkey. His reconciliation with Julius II took place in Bologna, which the warrior Pope had entered in triumph. Here Michelangelo received the order for a statue of his patron for the façade of San Petronio. It was to be larger than life size and cast in bronze. It was calculated that this gigantic statue would weigh no less than 18,000 pounds. The vicissitudes of the casting took up the whole tormented summer of 1507. On February 21 of the following year it was unveiled. The face of the Pontiff, severely majestic, was intended to instill the fear of God in citizens of Bologna and to discourage them from rebelling. Vain hope, for in 1511 upon the return of the former lord of Bologna, Giovanni Bentivoglio, the colossus was torn down by the embattled citizenry.

RIVALRIES: LEONARDO AND RAPHAEL

Left: Detail from the "Deluge": A father carrying his swooning son to safety. The influence of this group is plain in Raphael's fresco (below) in the Vatican rooms, which shows the Trojan hero Aeneas as he leaves his house, carrying his father on his back; his young son walks beside him.

Upon his return to Rome, Michelangelo found that Julius II was no longer interested in his tomb. He had decided, instead, to have Michelangelo do the decorations on the ceiling of the Sistine Chapel. The request, flattering though it appeared, aroused smoldering rebellion in his breast. He looked upon it as a maneuver by his enemies to rob him of the most ambitious work of his life, the papal mausoleum. He did not in fact lack enemies. His harsh manner and contrariness created them wherever he went. His rivalry with Leonardo da Vinci went back to Florentine days; it had been exacerbated by their contest for the frescoes in the Great Council Hall of the Palazzo Vecchio. But it really stemmed from the incompatibility of two diametrically opposed temperaments. In Rome, he found himself confronted by Bramante's clique and later by a compatriot of his, Raphael Sanzio. "All the misunderstandings that sprang up betwen Pope Julius and myself," Michelangelo was to write in his old age, "were caused by the envy of Bramante and of Raphael of Urbino who wanted to ruin me; and this was the reason I did not finish the tomb during his lifetime." In reality Raphael's feelings toward Michelangelo were a mixture of envy and admiration. "What there was of art in him he had from me," the sculptor said later of his dead young rival.

Above left: Engraving made from a reconstruction of Michelangelo's supposed cartoon for the "Battle of Cascina." The Signoria, after the banishment of the Medici and the reestablishment of the Republic, had decided to celebrate the victorious wars of the Commune against Pisa by having frescoes painted for their Great Council Hall. The episode shown occurred just before the battle fought in July, 1365, when the Florentine soldiers, overcome by the heat, were bathing in the Arno River at Cascina, on the outskirts of Pisa. Then, suddenly alarmed by the report that the Pisan forces were approaching, the soldiers hurriedly pulled their clothes on. Despite the surprise, they routed the enemy. Bottom left: Leonardo's sketch for a second fresco in the same Council room. This was to have shown the battle of Anghiari, another Florentine victory. Neither fresco was ever completed. The sketches for them were broken up, borrowed, copied and ultimately disappeared altogether.

BRAMANTE: A BITTER FEUD

Michelangelo's bitterest enemy was Donato Bramante of Urbino. Solidly entrenched in the papal court, winner of the contest for the remodeling of St. Peter's, the architect viewed with suspicion the two Florentines, Michelangelo and Sansovino. He thought that the Pontiff's whole interest and all the money available should be devoted to the rebuilding of St. Peter's. He had already begun the work of demolition on the medieval basilica and had done it with such open disregard for the works of art it contained that in some quarters of the Vatican he was known as the "Demolisher." Michelangelo did not hesitate to criticize this vandalic approach to reconstruction. He cordially reciprocated Bramante's dislike of him and insisted that the latter was responsible for persuading the Pope to drop the plans for his tomb. According to Michelangelo, Bramante had reiterated so many times that it was bad luck to think of one's burial when one was still alive, that Julius II had turned his attention to other projects. Actually the reasons for the Pope's change of mind were more complicated: Foremost was the certainty that the remodeling of the basilica would cast greater glory on him in the eyes of posterity than would the building of his own personal tomb. An even more compelling reason was the Pope's burning desire to free

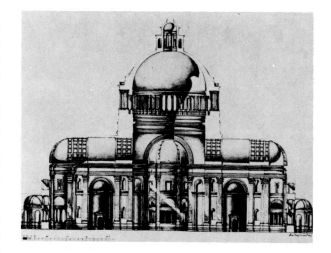

Italy from foreign interference. It was said of this warrior-Pope, the embodiment of the Church Militant, that he had thrown the keys of St. Peter into the Tiber in order to use only the sword of St. Paul. Meantime the rivalry between the two artists continued unabated, and the air was thick with charges and countercharges. Michelangelo knew that his rival liked to live in a lordly manner, which Bramante did, often spending beyond his means. When Michelangelo was working, his way of life was frugal to the point of squalor. He was content, in order to save time, to make do with bread and wine and to share his bed with his assistants. Bramante, on the other hand, found the Vatican allowance insufficient, and it was said that to make it do he used inferior materials for the new walls of the Belvedere (gallery and court in the Vatican) and for St. Peter's, and made them less thick than they ought to have been. Perhaps he knew

that his rival was aware of these irresponsible arrangements and feared a denunciation that might make him lose the direction of the great works.

In any event it would have been a relief to see Michelangelo leave Rome. As for the work in the Sistine Chapel, it is not certain whether Bramante tried to dissuade the Pope from entrusting it to Michelangelo, or whether he had an ulterior motive in encouraging his candidacy. Such a plan would have assured Michelangelo's downfall. If he refused the task, no one could have saved him from the Pontiff's wrath; if he accepted, he would never be able to withstand so exhausting a job, and his lack of experience in painting frescoes would make him lose Julius II's regard. Should this occur, a substitute was at hand: Raphael, the compatriot and favorite of Donato Bramante. Whether or not this plot really was brewed, it was a fact that in Vatican circles everyone knew how much importance the Pope attached to the work in the Sistine Chapel. The Chapel was a family affair. Its creator had in fact been another Della Rovere pope, Sixtus IV, in the second half of the 15th century. The frescoes on the walls had been done by famous painters: Ghirlandaio, Botticelli, Perugino (Raphael's teacher) and Luca Signorelli who had been one of Michelangelo's early inspirations. The decorations on the vaulted ceiling, however, had been done by a mediocre painter, Pier Matteo Serdenti d'Amelia, according to a medieval plan which showed a blue sky studded with bright stars. Julius II thought poorly of this ceiling in comparison with the rest. And so the redecoration was entrusted to Michelangelo. Bramante's plot—if there really was one—was destined to turn into Michelangelo's greatest triumph. The future, furthermore, was reserving him an even more spectacular revenge on Bramante. Almost half a century later Michelangelo was summoned by another pope, Paul III, to become director of the reconstruction of St. Peter's. He used his rival's original design of a central plan but made certain modifications, crowning it with the grandiose cupola which was to be forever connected with his name and with the monumental profile of the Eternal City.

THE GENIUS OF AN AGE

Leonardo: "Study for a Head"

Donatello: "David"

B. Cellini: "Perseus"

Michelangelo admired Donatello for his modernity and skill, but he criticized him for not putting the finishing touches on his statues. He had only unreserved praise for Ghiberti's doors to the Baptistry (in Florence) which he described as being "fit for paradise." To Cellini he wrote: "For years I have looked upon you as the greatest goldsmith that ever lived, and now I realize you are as great a sculptor." Although Bramante was his rival, he recognized and praised his skill as an architect for his work on St. Peter's. He also expressed, clearly and succinctly, his opinion of some of the painters of the period. He betrayed a lively distaste for Perugino, the teacher of Raphael, and said in public that he considered him "clumsy in art." His opinion of Francia was similar. He said to a son of the latter, a handsome youth, that his father was better at making "living figures than painted ones." He looked kindly upon Andrea del Sarto, about whom he said to Raphael that if he had been commissioned to do big things, as had Raphael, he, Raphael would have something to worry about. He also thought well of Pontormo: "If he lives and continues (to paint), he will reach heaven with his art." He prized Titian's colors and manner, but he did not hesitate to say he couldn't draw. Of Bronzino, who thought painting superior to sculpture, he said he "couldn't reason as well as a maidservant."

Andrea del Sarto: "Virgin with Chi[ld]"

Ghiberti: "The Annunciation"

D. Bramante:
"The Man with a Halberd"

Titian: Cardinal
"Hippolitus de' Medici"

Perugino: "Madonna and Angels"

Sebastiano del Piombo:
"Detail of the Resurrection of Lazarus"

Raphael: "Study for a Head"

Pontormo: "Alexander de' Medici"

Sebastiano del Piombo: "Young Man"

F. Francia: Detail from the Adoration

Bronzino: "Cosimo I de' Medici"

*Below: Plan of the vaulted ceiling
of the Sistine Chapel. Michelangelo
worked at it from 1509 to 1512.
Opposite page: The wall at
the end of the same chapel, on
which the artist painted, from
1533 to 1541, the dramatic fresco
"The Last Judgment,"
one of the greatest works ever created
by the genius of man.*

FOUR YEARS OF TORTURE: THE CEILING OF THE SISTINE CHAPEL

Has any man ever been kept for four years on a rack? Head bent back in such a way that his nape became a narrow crevasse between the back of his head and his spine; his beard and chin raised while the muscles of his neck swelled and stretched like a rope; his shoulders aching, his arms exhausted from being held straight up; his face reduced to a grotesque mask by the drops of paint that rained on it; and beneath him a chasm 65 feet deep? This was the position of Michelangelo while he painted the frescoes of the Sistine Chapel: four years of uninterrupted physical torment as well as deep spiritual wear and tear. At the time of the contract and the first sketches, the artist was 34. His ideas on frescoes probably went back to the days of his apprenticeship with Ghirlandaio in Santa Maria Novella. He had never really taken to this particular technique, which requires long experience, because a fresco must be done quickly without interruptions and without changes. The chapel was to contain not one single fresco but a whole cycle of frescoes large enough to cover the vaulted ceiling of an enormous chapel about 132 feet by 45 feet. But Michelangelo accepted the challenge of men and things; and the creative energy with which he threw himself into his work was characteristic of his heroic approach to life. The contract was signed in May, 1508. Immediately thereafter Michelangelo started to make sketches and cartoons; meantime workers prepared the ceiling by roughly plastering it. On this was put a finish coat of plaster on which, when still damp, a part of the sketch was transferred. Then it was painted with finely ground pigments mixed with water which were sucked into the plaster to become an integral part of the surface. It was slow work. The "Deluge," for example, took 32 days. By the end of 1508 the preparations had been completed. The helpers who were to collaborate in the great work had arrived from Florence (he didn't trust Roman ones who, he thought, were not sufficiently well-trained): Giuliano Bugiardini, Agnolo di Donnino, Jacopo l'Indaco and Bastiano, Sangallo's nephew. The frescoes were started at the beginning of January, 1509.

ARRIVAL OF THE LORD, BORNE ON THE WIND

In the first four central panels of the Sistine Chapel ceiling, the Lord, with His cloak billowing about Him, His white hair blowing by the speed of His movements, His hands stretched out in a gesture of creation, is separating light from darkness, land from water. He is creating the sun and the moon and growing things; He summons man to life from the mud and woman from man. The God of the Sistine Chapel, the God of "Genesis," is strangely reminiscent, in His features, of Julius II. He has the same furrowed brow, hoary beard, imperious expression.

The Pope spurred on the work: Old as he was he did not hesitate to venture up a ladder to the scaffolding to inspect the progress. Every so often there was a flare-up. One day, goaded beyond endurance by Michelangelo's usual laconic response of "As soon as I can!" to his question of "How much longer?" the Pope struck him with his staff. The artist, who had also just asked permission to visit his family in Florence, left the Chapel and returned to his house to pack his belongings. In the midst of his preparations, one of the Pope's intimates arrived with 500 ducats and the papal apologies. Michelangelo accepted the money, the apologies, and went to Florence.

These three paintings of God the Father as He created the world are parts of episodes of the Old Testament which are illustrated in the central panel of the Sistine ceiling.
Below: God creating the sun and the moon.
Upper right: God separating the waters from the earth.
Below: God giving life to Adam whose body was formed of mud. These scenes and the six others of the cycle were inspired by the Bible and can be divided into three groups. The first deals with the creation of the world, the second with the creation of mankind, the third with the origin of sin and its consequences.

*Below: The prophet Jonah,
one of the 12 seers
(five Sybils and seven Prophets)
who sit enthroned at the
base of the vault. Jonah, who
spent three days inside the whale,
is the symbol of Christ whose
resurrection took place
on the third day. He is the
only one in this series who
looks toward God.*

A WORLD OF GIANTS

The Vatican treasury paid only irregularly; this was typical of Renaissance courts. By all accounts Michelangelo administered his funds wisely and prudently. Thirty ducats a month were enough for his modest personal needs. He gave 15 to his assistants who often shared their master's meager supper. Jacopo l'Indaco, whose cheerful and clownish disposition served as a counterfoil to Michelangelo's touchy gloom, was the most frequent guest. In addition to salaries, there was the outlay of money for pigments and plaster. After the running expenses had been taken care of, the rest of the money was set aside and found its way to Florence. This mode of life did not leave much time or money for feasting; but Michelangelo had long since caught the Florentine habit of parsimony. The lordly airs that Bramante, Raphael and their followers gave themselves at court amused him. He himself cared so little about his personal appearance that even the modest cost of stockings seemed superfluous to him. For months on end, day and night, he wore cheap boots over his bare feet; when he finally got around to taking them off, bits of the soles of his feet came off with them. These are the economies of a man who gives much thought to his family. Michelangelo, solitary by nature, never wanted to marry; but from his father's house there came a steady stream of requests for help. From the time that the eldest Buonarroti boy locked himself up in a monastery, Michelangelo felt the weight of the responsibility for the younger ones, especially since his father could not be counted upon for much. He too did nothing but ask for money and suggest investments. Of the remaining brothers, Buonarroto, Giovan Simone and Gismondo, the first was Michelangelo's favorite. An illness of his in 1510 worried Michelangelo so much that he very nearly dropped everything to rush to Florence, risking another outburst of papal temper. But he was generous with the others as well, sending them money, and filling his letters to them with advice and admonitions. His letters were just like him: affectionate and angry at the same time. While he painted his powerful characters on the vast ceiling, his Florentine family was ever present with their needs, their quarrels; and perhaps it was they who kept him human in his world of giants.

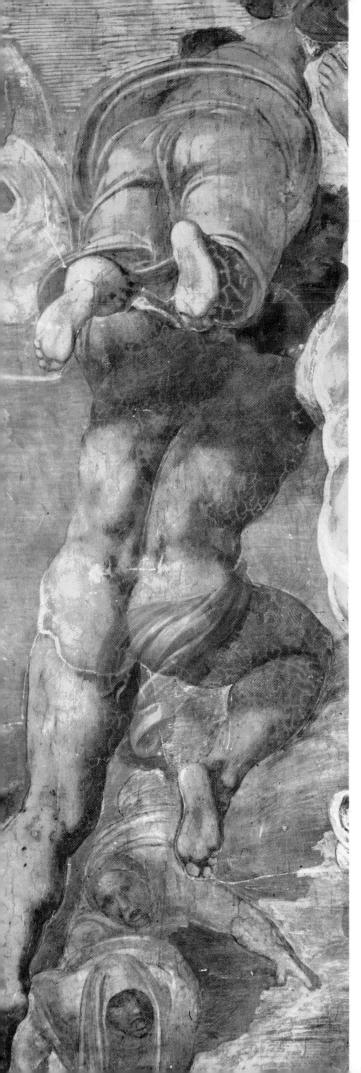

BODIES BLOWN BY THE WINDS OF CATASTROPHE

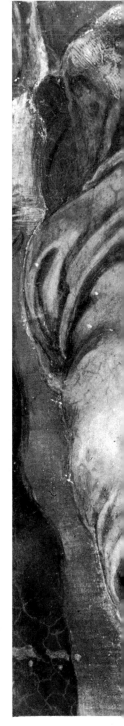

Toward the end of four years of torture, during which he had held his head back and his eyes heavenward, Michelangelo had lost the habit of looking straight ahead or down. In order to read a letter or a notation he had to raise it over his head. Tension, physical and mental, had been constant and experienced in the most complete spiritual solitude. "I am much troubled and physically exhausted; I have no friends, nor do I want any," he once wrote his brother Buonarroto. Every once in a while the Pope would turn up with his ever-lasting question: When will the work be done? The reply remained unchanged: "When I can." One day—it was then the fall of 1512—Julius II, at the end of his endurance, threatened to have the artist thrown off the scaffolding. Perhaps Michelangelo was secretly waiting for this outburst of temper as a signal. He ordered the scaffolding to be taken down and on October 31, 1512, the completed ceiling was uncovered. The next day, at the solemn mass of All Saints Day, there took place the official inauguration accompanied by the music of a glorious *Te Deum*, a hymn of Thanksgiving. To the crowd of onlookers was suddenly revealed a vision so splendid as to be staggering: The gigantic world of the Sistine Chapel with its Sybils and Prophets facing one another over the abyss of the future, surrounded on all sides by powerful figures who were the incarnation of a dream of plastic perfection. The whole was held together by the frightening lessons pried loose from the stories of the Old Testament. Never again was a *Te Deum* to be sung for so signal a victory in art. The closest to it came 29 years later, again on All Saints Day, 1541, when the great altar wall was unveiled, and the haunting vision of the "Last Judgment" appeared to the faithful. In this last fresco, executed when he was at the threshold of old age, Michelangelo added to his earlier masterpiece—whose inspiration he had drawn from chapters of the Old Testament—another one, drawn this time from the most terrifying page of the New Testament. Here, translated by him into color and form, teeming bodies are blown about by the winds of catastrophe, huge foreshortened figures are flung with a force great enough to crumble the walls, while others, paralyzed with fear, await eternal damnation. And in the center, the figure of Christ the Judge dominates the turmoil. But in 1512 the "Last Judgment" was still far distant, hovering within the shadows of the future; perhaps only the great Sybils had foreseen it.

Below and opposite page: Three powerful figures from the "Last Judgment." In this fresco, which covers almost 200 square meters, the entire altar wall at the back of the Sistine Chapel, Michelangelo used new techniques of foreshortening. For example, he had the wall lined with a thin layer of bricks so that it slanted inward, as it rose, some nine inches in a total height of 48 feet. This was intended as an aid to visibility and as a protection against the settling of dust. For the plaster he mixed lime with powdered clay instead of with sand, thus giving it a hard smooth surface. When the fresco was uncovered, not all voices were raised in praise. Pietro Aretino, for example, described it as a "bunch of nudes," implying that it looked indecent. The writer had not forgiven Michelangelo for having ignored his advice on the "Last Judgment," nor had he forgotten his vain request for a drawing as a present.

THE TERRIBLE OLD MEN

The dreams which Michelangelo had dreamt so long for the tomb of Julius II took form and substance in the decoration of the Sistine Chapel. Indeed his plans—of which there remain drawings—provided for the placement, around the base of the mausoleum, of a mighty guard of honor: the Sybils, those pagan seers of the future, and the Prophets, heralds of the Messiah among the Israelites. Of these giants, filled with the breath of the Divine Spirit, only one came to see the light of day in the form of a statue: Moses. The others can be found on the ceiling of the Sistine Chapel, poring over immense books in which are contained the secrets of future ages, or they are in a state of suspension, listening for a celestial message. All his life Michelangelo was attracted by the mystery of those seers who found traces of the presence of God in the history of mankind. It was for this reason that he wanted to set up their marble effigies to guard the tomb of his great and awesome pontiff. But the true monument to Julius II was to consist in having his memory forever linked to the Sistine Chapel. And the Pope's impatience was not after all misplaced, for he scarcely had time to see the finished ceiling. Death overtook him on February 21, 1513, less than four months after the *Te Deum* which greeted the completion of the vast cycle of frescoes. His successor was the son of Lorenzo the Magnificent, Cardinal Giovanni de' Medici, who took the name of Leo X. The new pope as a boy had sat at his father's dinner table beside Michelangelo. But it was not until two years after his accession to the papacy that he remembered his existence. Leo X, who had a real predilection for Raphael, was uneasily aware in Michelangelo's presence of the artist's stormy greatness.

Left: Very different indeed from the young athlete pictured in the scene of the "Creation" is the aged Adam who looks up to Christ in the "Last Judgment." Right: The prophet Ezekiel, one of the major biblical prophets, who sees God on a chariot of fire. This figure has often been thought to be another of the many portraits of Pope Julius II.

THE MYSTERY OF THE PROPHECIES

The sight of the severe figures of the Sybils, with their deeply lined faces, whose foreboding of the anguish of the years to come is already stamped upon their countenances, makes it easy to understand the feeling of alarm that rose in Leo X in the presence of Michelangelo's volcanic genius. His own outlook on life was quite different from the artist's, as was indeed that of the Roman world in which he lived. It is doubtful if the men of the Renaissance understood the harsh lesson Michelangelo tried to teach. If they did understand, they cannot have liked it. His awareness of the tragedy of life struck a discord in their illusions of happiness and well-being. However, Leo X, like his father before him, was a competent judge of talent. Uncomfortable as Michelangelo's personality made him, he nevertheless decided to entrust to him the execution of the façade of San Lorenzo in Florence. This was the church most closely connected with the House of Medici from the time that the founders of the family fortunes had paid hard cash for its restoration as a burial place. At one time the Pope had thought to turn to Giuliano da Sangallo, but his illness and death in 1516 cleared the way for Michelangelo. The latter, however, looked upon this new commission as a burden, because it forced him to go back on his contract with the Della Rovere family for the tomb of Julius II; hence his obstinate resistance. But Pope Leo would not listen to reason. The sculptor began again his trips to the Apuan Alps in search of marbles for the basilica, and after a series of projects, each more elaborate than the preceding one, the plan for the façade took form.

On this page and the next:
Two paintings of Sybils. Female
equivalents of the Prophets,
they were the great seers of
pagan antiquity. On this page: The
Cumaean Sybil who, in her majestic
old age, symbolizes the age and
the strength of the Church of
Rome. According to legend she
sold to Tarquin the Superb three
books of prophecy for the price he
had asked for nine; she then
burned the remaining ones.
Next page: The thoughtful profile
of the Persian Sybil.

A GRAVE FOR
FOUR GREAT MEN

There were two interested parties in the rebuilding of San Lorenzo: first, the Pope, son of Lorenzo the Magnificent, then close to him, another Medici also in the Vatican, Cardinal Giulio, illegitimate son of Lorenzo the Magnificent's murdered brother. This prelate seemed to take even more interest than did the Pope in the project for the façade. To this, besides the traditional Tuscan geometric divisions of the pediment, there was to be added an unprecedentedly complex group of statues: a kind of "sacred colloquy" between the most revered saints of the church, on the one hand, and the leaders of the Medici family on the other. This was the grandiose program put forth by Cardinal Giulio. According to Michelangelo it was to have been "of architecture and sculpture the mirror of all Italy." For a variety of reasons, some of them political, the project was abandoned, and all Michelangelo's magnificent schemes came to nothing. In 1520 the contract signed two years earlier was annulled, and the artist received from the same patrons a new commission. He was to build inside San Lorenzo a funerary chapel destined to receive the remains of four members of the Medici family: Giuliano and Lorenzo the Magnificent, and the two descendants named after them: Giuliano, Duke of Nemours, and Lorenzo, Duke of Urbino. Michelangelo had grown accustomed to sudden changes of plans on the part of his patrons ever since the days of Julius II. The project for a new funerary monument appealed to him, for his spirit was always attuned to the apotheosis of death. There was already in San Lorenzo a funerary chapel for the first Medici, "The Old Sacristy," in which Donatello and Verrocchio left eloquent testimonials of their genius. Michelangelo was not afraid of measuring himself against these masters.

Right: A dizzying view, taken from above, of the Medici Chapel: The entrance is in the wall opposite the altar where the unfinished tombs of the two brothers Giuliano and Lorenzo de' Medici are located. Above these is the statue of Mary with the Babe and St. Cosimo and St. Damiano. To the right, as one enters, is the tomb of Lorenzo, Duke of Urbino; opposite it is that of the Duke of Nemours.

VACANT STARE OF THE GODS

The "New Sacristy" of San Lorenzo, as the Medici funerary chapel came to be known, is perhaps Michelangelo's greatest work in stone. Here, for the first and only time, he was able to give his statues a proper setting. The sculpture and architecture so perfectly complement each other that they form a harmonious and powerfully expressive unity. This work, so apparently coherent in its inspiration, underwent in the course of its realization a number of painful alterations: Started, then interrupted because of political events, taken up again later and finally abandoned, it nonetheless remains one of Michelangelo's most important works. Pope Leo saw only the first stages of the concentrated preliminary labor; he died unexpectedly in 1521. Thereafter the responsibility for the continuation of the chapel fell entirely on Cardinal Giulio de' Medici. The new Pope, a Flemish one, who took the name of Adrian VI, had no interest in art; quite the contrary, for he seemed to think that churchmen devoted far too much of their attention to it to the detriment of their true task as vicars of Christ. His election was looked upon as a calamity by the artists who frequented the Vatican, which was only confirmed by his zeal in having the courtyard of the Belvedere closed so that the nakedness of the pagan statues could no longer shock visitors. Michelangelo heard only the echoes of these doings. He was in Florence, absorbed in the work on the Chapel. It was to be the only Renaissance monument in which the pagan concept of the exaltation of the deceased and the Christian concept of the immortality of the soul appeared harmoniously fused. Very soon news from the Vatican created an atmosphere of good feeling in the Medici entourage. The austere Pope, Adrian VI, died after only two years of reign, and Cardinal Giulio succeeded him. During a visit of the new Pope, who chose the name of Clement VII, Michelangelo was urged to speed up his work. The Pontiff would not have been displeased to have had two tombs added to those already planned for: one for his cousin Leo X and the other for himself. He too felt slightly uneasy in the presence of the artist. It was said that he never sat down in his presence for fear Michelangelo might do the same. However he made him an allowance of 50 ducats a month in addition to giving him a house near San Lorenzo, and continually prodded him with letters. "You know," he wrote sadly, "that Popes do not live very long. . . ."

Far left: The tombs of the Dukes
in the New Sacristy of San
Lorenzo. The first one is of Lorenzo
the Magnificent's third son,
Giuliano, Duke of Nemours,
who symbolizes action; at his feet
are the statues of Night and Day.
The second tomb is that
of Lorenzo II, Duke of Urbino,
the son of Piero, the first
born son and heir of Lorenzo
the Magnificent. Duke Lorenzo's
pose represents Thought.
At his feet are the statues of
Twilight and Dawn. On this page
are closeups of the faces of
the two dukes who, dressed as
Roman warriors, are transfigured
and made to look like
demi-gods. The sculptor here
made no attempt to portray the
dukes as they really were.

"THEN WAKE ME NOT"

The statues on the Medici tombs are shrouded in beauty and mystery. Over the course of centuries their spiritual content has been the subject of endless controversy and still today is open to conjecture. What is the meaning of the allegories of Day and Night, Dawn and Twilight on the tombs of the two generals dressed as ancient Romans? Did they symbolize Time which devours all things? Did they represent the spiritual triumph of the deceased over the transitoriness of earthly things? And why are the covers of the sarcophagi in the form of broken arcs? Was this for aesthetic or religious considerations? A partial interpretation is suggested by Michelangelo himself in a note on the back of a drawing: "Night and Day are speaking and say: We have, in our swift course, led Duke Giuliano to his death; it is only just that he take his revenge as he does. And his revenge is this: Since we have led him to his end, now that he is dead, by our doing, he has extinguished our light, and our eyes no longer shine upon the earth." The artist appears to see death from a pagan point of view, with all nature in mourning for the deceased. It may well be, as some believe, that the statues in the chapel are an expression of Michelangelo's pessimism. Indeed Michelangelo never finished his project for the chapel, nor did he even finish some of the statues he had begun. During this period the second revolt of the Florentines against Medici tyranny took place. The republic was restored and the city besieged. Michelangelo participated in these events with fiery enthusiasm. The return of the Medici, with the shattering of all hopes for the liberty of his city, filled his heart with a sadness that was reflected in his sculptures. The famous four lines he composed later about Night punctuate this dejection. The sleeping woman had aroused the admiration of contemporaries, that of the humanist Giovanni Strozzi in particular. In a mediocre four line verse he expressed the idea that if she were awakened she would speak. In her name, Michelangelo retorted bitterly: "My sleep is dear to me, but dearer to me still is being made of stone, for so long as ruin and shame endure, it is a boon to hear naught, to see naught: So wake me not, speak softly."

Far left: Dawn. Her pose, like Twilight's, was inspired by the allegories of the river gods on the arch of Septimius Severus in Rome. The veil on her head and the band below her breasts have been interpreted as symbols of mourning and grief.
Above: The famous Night, with the darkling emblems of an owl and a mask of trageay.
Left: Twilight. These figures, begun around 1524, were completed around 1531.

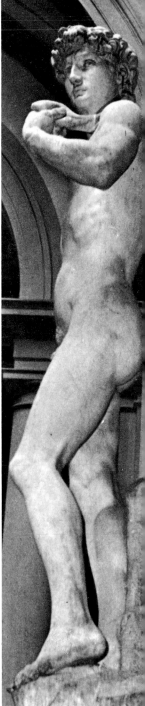

THE GLORIFICATION
OF MAN

However frequently signs of pessimism may appear in Michelangelo, this feeling never led him into sterile desolation. On the contrary, it made him face life boldly. It was this attitude which led him to the exaltation of man which is apparent in his most expressive works. The cultural atmosphere of the Renaissance, which places man in the center of the universe, is not alien to such a heroic concept, but in Michelangelo the process becomes internal. Physical beauty becomes the reflection of an innate harmony. This may be inspired by Dante who looked upon perfection, physical and moral as a "ladder to the Divine," as a means of approaching the Creator. The artist's powerful figures, full of an extraordinary vitality and suggestive of the full capacity for action of the character portrayed, appear to be actors in a divine play. They are not recognizable as actual individuals. Michelangelo, hating portraits, withdrew his characters from the world of material things. He retorted to those who asked him why he had idealized Giuliano and Lorenzo de'Medici to the point of making them unrecognizable: "Who will remember their faces in a thousand years?" In this way his characters no longer belong to history; they are, in a certain sense, sculptured for eternity.

Far left: Close-up of the "David"; next to it, a full view of the statue. It was carved by Michelangelo out of a marble block that had first been used by Simone da Fiesole for the statue of a giant. The work, however, had been interrupted because it was not going well, and the partially chiseled block had remained in the courtyard of the works of the Cathedral of Florence to be used for something else. Michelangelo, who had been told of it by friends, decided to put in a request for it from the workers and from the Gonfalonier Pier Soderini whose friendly patronage he enjoyed. Having obtained the block in 1501, and having undertaken to carve a statue from it within a maximum of two years, he prepared a wax model of the youthful David with a sling in his hand. The meaning of the

statue was not only religious but also political. Indeed, it pointed to the duty of the rulers of Florence to protect liberty and to govern wisely as David had done for the people of Israel. After the marble statue was finished, the Signory (the ruling body of Florence) called together a great meeting of artists to decide on the best place for the "David." The majority voted for the entrance to the Palazzo Vecchio (the Old Palace) to replace Donatello's "Judith." It was transported there the following April by means of a massive rigging on rollers. Above: Another example, this one from the frescoes on the ceiling of the Sistine Chapel, of Michelangelo's glorification of the human form: Adam in the "Creation of Man."

MAN'S GRIEF

Above and right, two important groups from the vast and dramatic panel, one of the nine, on the ceiling of the Sistine Chapel, the "Deluge." Above: Two superimposed heads, of a father and son, the latter fainting, as the father tries to carry him to safety. Right: A group of fugitives before the fury of the waters and the force of the winds. Their violence can be inferred from the bent tree. The group occupies the left side of the fresco which was the

first one Michelangelo painted during 32 days of work. Immediately after he had finished it, the artist, to whom this technique was still new, saw with consternation that the paint was flecked here and there with mold. Michelangelo was so discouraged he wanted to give up altogether. But Sangallo, a good friend, suggested that he use less water in the mixture and this proved a solution.

All Michelangelo's creatures appear to be heavily burdened with the legacy of grief which the sons of Adam inherited. It is in this psychological approach that the profound difference between Michelangelo's world and that of the Ancients' lies. Their serenity is unknown to him. In fact his heroes, his demigods, are shackled by servitude to grief and sin and by their awareness of their condition. Sometimes the contemplation of individual unhappiness expands into a larger vision of cosmic disaster, as in the "Deluge" or later in the "Last Judgment." Even the gentle emotions which comfort man in his loneliness are seen by Michelangelo in a dramatic light; Mother love is indicative of neither peace nor gentleness. The Madonna over Lorenzo the Magnificent's tomb seems not to see the Babe clutching her breast: Her gaze appears lost in a painful meditation. The same holds true for the young mother (far right) in the "Deluge"; she hardly notices the infant anxiously clinging to her leg as though it were the trunk of a tree. The gesture with which she clutches in her arms the younger child has something animalistic rather than human about it, her face, in the shelter of the cloak swollen by the winds like a ship's sail, is grim and desperate. The torment of the artist is undoubtedly reflected in the torment of his creations. Michelangelo knows all the bitterness of life: the meanness of his family, the ingratitude of rulers, the hatred of rivals, the loneliness of the heart. He also knows the mortification of physical miseries: ugliness and sickness. To the end of his days he was in poor health, subject to attacks of nerves. Sometimes he was brought to the very brink of death by painful infirmities. But more devastating than his physical afflictions were his spiritual ones. His only escape was work, and he shut himself up in it as a monk does in his cell, skipping meals, stealing hours from his sleep, cutting himself off from everybody. In order to work at night he devised an odd headgear to which he affixed a candle made from goat grease, which dripped less than wax. In this way he avoided the necessity of constantly moving the light as he worked. The vacillating flame among the ghostly statues made fantastic patterns of lights and shadows.

MICHELANGELO'S
PRIVATE LIFE

A reputation for gloominess was the natural result of the sense of grief which underlies so much of Michelangelo's artistic work. And yet a close study of his daily life reveals moments when this perverse, difficult, solitary man enjoyed life in ordinary ways: an evening spent convivially, happy faces around the dinner table, well-chosen wines, affectionate voices. "Last night," he wrote to Sebastiano del Piombo, "our captain friend Cuio and some other gentlemen graciously invited me to dine with them, which gave me great pleasure, for it took me a little out of my melancholy or my madness. . . ." Even when he again became a prey to melancholy, at least there had been a momentary respite from it, and the pleasure of the recollection remained.

Michelangelo's character was undoubtedly a tormented one, bordering on the neurotic. He liked to shroud himself in mystery, and he often spoke of frightful traps set for him by his rivals. These were not always imaginary, for he really did have enemies, artists consumed with envy and noblemen infuriated by his spirit of independence. Duke Alexander de' Medici, for example—the one whose return to Florence was made possible by the help of a large army after the siege of 1530—never forgave Michelangelo for having joined the Florentine rebels and would have had him killed had it not been for the protection of the Pope. The last straw was that Michelangelo had had the impudence to say that the Medici Palace ought to have been razed to the ground, and the space left called Piazza de' Muli (Mule Square)—a biting allusion to the illegitimate origins of the duke and of many members of his family, including the Pope. Although he was critical of others, Michelangelo, true Florentine that he was, did not spare himself. It probably kept him from succumbing to his black moods. During one of the most tormented periods of his life, while he was painting the Sistine Chapel ceiling, he poked fun at himself in a sonnet by describing the incongruous positions he was forced to take to do his work. Later, when he was an old man living in a squalid house, he wrote another poem in which he jokingly enumerated his discomforts, among them the presence of a large number of hard-working spiders who had turned his dwelling into a "spinning mill."

Opposite page: Sonnet with a sketch of himself painting the Sistine Chapel. The original is in the Laurentian Library in Florence, another of Michelangelo's architectural works. It was commissioned by Pope Clement VII and is considered a masterpiece.

Left: A menu with the courses illustrated by Michelangelo. This curious document is also in the Laurentian Library. Below: A sketch by the artist for the frescoes in the Pauline Chapel. This was his last painting. He worked on it around 1550. The original sketch is in the Louvre.

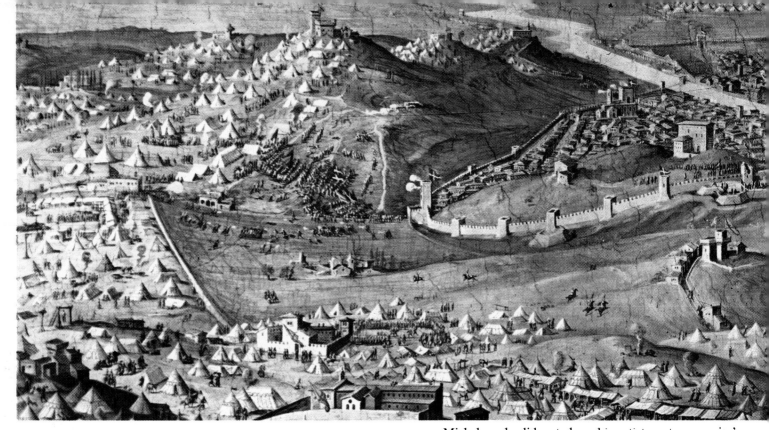

REBEL AND DESERTER

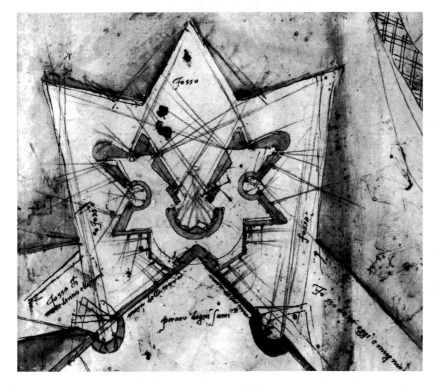

Michelangelo did not share his artist contemporaries' political apathy. They were content to find a patron who would look after them; he, on the other hand, cared deeply about the fate of his beloved Florence. When the city rebelled against the Medici, he threw himself wholeheartedly into the fray. In 1527, when news of the sack of Rome reached Florence, and her citizens heard of the difficulties in which Clement VII, the Medici Pope, had become embroiled, riots broke out. The two petty little Medici tyrants, Alexander and Hyppolitus, were soon forced to take flight together with the cardinal who was regent. With their departure the republic, which had collapsed in 1512, was reinstated and Niccolò Capponi made gonfalonier (chief official of the state). However the wind soon changed: the Pope came to an agreement with the Austrian Emperor at the expense of Florence, and the city prepared itself for a siege. On April 6, 1529, Michelangelo was made governor-general and put in charge of defense. But then in the summer he was sent to inspect the fortifications of other nearby cities and it soon became apparent that the authorities wanted to get rid of him. The Gonfalonier disapproved of his plans for defense; Malatesta Baglioni, commander of the army, disliked him intensely; and others suspected him outright of conniving for the return of the Medici. Inevitably his situation became untenable, and his reaction was typical: he fled. He left the city on September 21 to go to Venice via Ferrara, with the thought of then accepting an invitation from the King of France. The Signory proclaimed him a rebel and a deserter, but continued to send delegations to him to urge his return. This may have been what Michelangelo wanted. Or perhaps despite his contempt for these men, he could not resist a call from his native city, caught in a siege and threatened by the plague. In November he returned and, until the last day of the desperate eight months that followed, he worked for the defense of freedom.

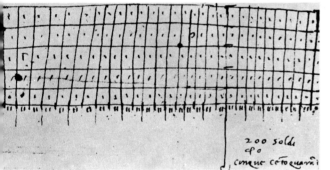

200 soldi
d o
c̄mąnc cetoquarni

Above: Vasari's fresco which adorns Clement VII's room in the Palazzo Vecchio in Florence. It is a panoramic view of the city, besieged by the Prince of Orange, showing the encampment of the enemy forces. Philibert of Orange was commander of the imperial troops sent by Charles V to return the Medici to power.

Left: This small drawing, in the Buonarroti museum in Florence, is a plan for the building operations carried out by Michelangelo for the fortifications of the city at the time of its unsuccessful defense against the Medici. Below: Two sketches of fortifications having to do with the works at the gates of the Prato d'Ognissanti.

THE EVENING STAR

On the fateful day of August 12, 1530, after betrayal turned the city over to the enemy, Michelangelo, from his hiding place in the tower of Saint Niccolò, saw the imperial and Medici troops occupy Florence. Certain that Duke Alexander would not hesitate to have him killed, he remained in hiding until an ordinance of Clement VII reassured him. On this occasion the Pope behaved like a real Medici, for in his eyes artistic worth transcended every other consideration. Indeed, he sent instructions that not one hair of Michelangelo's head was to be touched; furthermore, if the artist would again take up the work on the Medici Chapel where he had left off at the time of the rebellion, the original arrangements for money and accommodations could be restored to him. It was certainly a generous offer, and Michelangelo accepted it. But his mind had been permanently set against the Medici, and he went back to work on the tombs, "propelled more by fear than by affection." The death of Pope Clement in 1534 was to interrupt the work forever. In the same year, after having buried his 90-year-old father, Michelangelo left Florence, resolved never to return. He arrived in Rome exhausted, embittered, brooding about death. But life was clamoring for him: The new Pope, Paul III of the Farnese family, wanted him to finish the Sistine Chapel and, more important still, Vittoria Colonna came into his life. His friendship with her, which started in his late maturity, came like the evening star among the shadows of twilight. When they met, the artist was over 60 and the marchesa had passed 45. The bond between them lasted until her death 10 years later. It was a Platonic love, a deep spiritual affinity. Superficially, the two could not have been more different. He came from a modest Florentine middle-class family; she from the most patrician of Roman families, the House of Colonna. Michelangelo was solitary, difficult, introverted. He had no friends and claimed he wanted none; Vittoria, although she had retired from society, gathered about her a small court of intellectuals who vied with each other in singing her praises. Her admirers and correspondents included poets, philosophers, theologians, painters, statesmen. Among these latter was Baldassare Castiglione, author of the *Courtier*, a manual on "gracious living" which put forth standards of good behavior as well as the advantages of intellectual attainment. At the time of its publication in 1528 it became a best seller throughout western Europe and still today makes

Right: Portrait of Vittoria Colonna from an etching in the Bertarelli Collection in Milan. There is also another painting of her by the Venetian painter Sebastiano del Piombo. Michelangelo wanted to do one of her but for some reason was dissuaded from doing so. Nonetheless it seems that he did portray her in the woman wearing the yellow-orange veil at the feet of Mary in the fresco of the "Last Judgment." Vittoria responded to the artist's devotion with a sincere friendship. Although she addressed some of her poetry to other members of her circle of intellectual friends, she never wrote any to him. He, on the other hand, composed many sonnets for her. These make up the best-known portion of his poetic production. Left: Portraits by famous artists of some of the most outstanding members of Vittoria's literary circle. They are, from the top: Pietro Aretino, by Titian, a writer with a poisonous pen, who asked her for money and received good advice. Baldassare Castiglione, by Raphael, author of the famous Courtier, *the treatise on the ideal type of the Renaissance gentleman. Pietro Bembo, by Titian, a prelate and exquisite rhymester. Ludovico Ariosto, also by Titian, author of* Orlando Furioso (Roland's Madness).

for very good reading. Among Vittoria's friends there was also the venomous-tongued Pietro Aretino. Vittoria herself wrote mediocre poetry, pale imitations of Petrarch, which did not deter her friends from acclaiming her the greatest woman poet of the century—a somewhat safe statement as there were scarcely any other Italian women poets at the time. She was not particularly beautiful if one is to judge from her portraits, but there were those who sang praises of her physical beauty. "There are three wondrous gifts," wrote Paolo Giovo, "which Nature has bestowed upon this lady: eyes, hands, breasts, which form a beautiful harmony."

Dissimilar as they were, there existed between her and Michelangelo a kinship born of grief. When she was very young, Vittoria had been married to Francesco Ferrante d'Avalos, Marchese di Pescara, a military man. The marriage of convenience flowered unexpectedly, but for her only, into a marriage of love. Ferrante died from wounds received in battle, and from then on his widow lived in prayer and penance celebrating in her poetry the memory of her husband. His loss left Vittoria unconsolable just as Michelangelo remained unconsolable for the loss of Florentine liberty. Furthermore both were deeply concerned with religion and with the necessity for reform in the church. Michelangelo had remained a follower of the rebel Savonarola; Vittoria kept up with the most advanced currents of thought of the epoch; at times she even strayed in the direction of Protestantism. The artist admired the masculine vigor of her intellect: "A man, or rather a god, speaks through the mouth of a woman," he wrote in one of his poems inspired by the marchesa. Their conversations in the garden of Saint Sylvester at Montecavallo became a cherished habit for Michelangelo. Whenever he arrived, Vittoria would rise to go and meet him; then she made him sit next to her "in the garden, at the foot of a laurel leaning against the green ivy which covered the wall." It was thus that their contemporaries described them. When the marchesa died, on February 25, 1547, Michelangelo went to take his final leave of her as she lay on her death bed. He would have liked to kiss her forehead for the first and last time, but he didn't dare, so he limited himself to brushing her hand with his lips. In one of his letters Michelangelo wrote of the warmest affection of his life: "She was very fond of me and I of her; death has deprived me of a great friend."

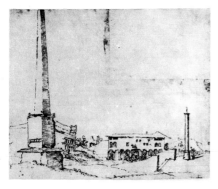

THE IMPRINT OF GENIUS

Above: Martin van Heemskerk's drawing of the Piazza del Campidoglio around 1536. The palaces (among them the 12th-century senatorial palace which was renovated in the 13th century) were built alongside statues and ruins. This drawing and others of the same place are to be found in the Cabinet of Designs in Berlin. It was Pope Paul III, of the Farnese family, who first conceived the idea of putting some order into the Capitoline area. Below: Stefano du Pérac's drawing of Michelangelo's plans for the Campidoglio. Three palaces, symmetrically disposed, enclose the square on three sides, leaving open the fourth side which looks out over the city in a terraced effect. Right: Night view of the Campidoglio which is a fine example of city planning.

One of Michelangelo's outstanding accomplishments in Rome, during the last thirty years of his life, was the remodeling of the Campidoglio. The Vatican authorities had been aware, for some time, that the medieval arrangement of the square was inadequate and that it offered an unfortunate contrast to the new look, elsewhere, of the city. Renovations were begun with the transfer, to the Capitoline area, of the statue of Marcus Aurelius. It was also in this square that on December 10, 1537, Michelangelo was granted Roman citizenship, along with other Roman artists, among whom was Titian. Michelangelo, who had been called in as a consultant, had the base of the statue changed from a rectangular one to an oval one, a shape more in harmony with the setting he already had in mind for the area. Unfortunately, "the magnificent and rich design," which Vasari reported Michelangelo had done, has been lost; only three partial sketches by the hand of the artist remain. However, the plan has come down to us through an engraving done in 1569. The access ramp to the top of the Capitoline Hill and the magnificent stairs to the Senatorial Palace were executed while he was still alive, but the final realization of the original plans underwent some alterations after Michelangelo's death.

It is a fitting tribute to Michelangelo that the two spiritual poles of Rome—Saint Peter's and the Campidoglio—should bear the unmistakable imprint of his genius.